GRIMMY

A BOOK OF POSTCARDS
BY MIKE PETERS

Pomegranate

SAN FRANCISCO

Pomegranate Communications, Inc.
Box 6099
Rohnert Park, CA 94927
www.pomegranate.com

Pomegranate Europe Ltd.
Fullbridge House, Fullbridge
Maldon, Essex CM9 4LE
England

ISBN 0-7649-0711-5
Pomegranate Catalog No. A527

Pomegranate publishes books of
postcards on a wide range of subjects.
Please write to the publisher for more information.

Designed by Shannon Lemme
Printed in Korea
07 06 05 04 03 02 01 00 99 98   10 9 8 7 6 5 4 3 2 1

To facilitate detachment of the postcards from this book, fold each card along its perforation line before tearing.

From one of the most popular cartoons in America, *Mother Goose and Grimm™,* comes doggy-devil Grimmy, that canine clown who careens through life like a furry, uncontrolled superball. Winner of the Reuben Award, this comic strip has been made into an animated children's television show and is currently syndicated in such widely diverse locations as Japan, Malaysia, Germany, Guyana, the Netherlands, the Phillipines, Finland, Norway, Sweden, Jamaica, Barbados, Saudi Arabia, China, and the Czech Republic.

The antics of the unconventional Grimmy are the creation of award-winning artist Mike Peters, recognized as one of the nation's most prominent cartoon artists for his political cartoons, his comic strips, and his television animation work. He is an editorial cartoonist for the Dayton (Ohio) *Daily News,* and his many honors include the Pulitzer Prize, the Sigma Delta Chi Award, and three Headliner Awards. He has also created *Peters' Postscripts,* animated editorial cartoons for NBC's *Nightly News,* and hosted the fourteen-part PBS television series, *The World of Cartooning with Mike Peters.*

Thirty of Grimmy's more notorious moments are presented for your amusement in this book of postcards.

GRIMMY from *Mother Goose and Grimm*
Illustration and text by Mike Peters

Pomegranate BOX 6099, ROHNERT PARK, CA 94927

GRIMMY from *Mother Goose and Grimm*
Illustration and text by Mike Peters

Pomegranate BOX 6099, ROHNERT PARK, CA 94027

GRIMMY from *Mother Goose and Grimm*
Illustration and text by Mike Peters

Pomegranate

BOX 6099, ROHNERT PARK, CA 94927

GRIMMY from *Mother Goose and Grimm*
Illustration and text by Mike Peters

Pomegranate BOX 6099, ROHNERT PARK, CA 94927

GRIMMY from *Mother Goose and Grimm*
Illustration and text by Mike Peters

BOX 6099, ROHNERT PARK, CA 94927

Pomegranate

GRIMMY from *Mother Goose and Grimm*
Illustration and text by Mike Peters

Pomegranate BOX 6099, ROHNERT PARK, CA 94927

GRIMMY from *Mother Goose and Grimm*
Illustration and text by Mike Peters

Pomegranate

BOX 6099, ROHNERT PARK, CA 94927

GRIMMY from *Mother Goose and Grimm*
Illustration and text by Mike Peters

Pomegranate BOX 6099, ROHNERT PARK, CA 94927

GRIMMY from *Mother Goose and Grimm*
Illustration and text by Mike Peters

Pomegranate   BOX 6099, ROHNERT PARK, CA 94927

GRIMMY from *Mother Goose and Grimm*
Illustration and text by Mike Peters

Pomegranate BOX 6099, ROHNERT PARK, CA 94927

GRIMMY from *Mother Goose and Grimm*
Illustration and text by Mike Peters

Pomegranate   BOX 6099, ROHNERT PARK, CA 94927

GRIMMY from *Mother Goose and Grimm*
Illustration and text by Mike Peters

Pomegranate BOX 6099, ROHNERT PARK, CA 94927

GRIMMY from *Mother Goose and Grimm*
Illustration and text by Mike Peters

Pomegranate BOX 6099, ROHNERT PARK, CA 94927

GRIMMY from *Mother Goose and Grimm*
Illustration and text by Mike Peters

Pomegranate   BOX 6099, ROHNERT PARK, CA 94927

GRIMMY from *Mother Goose and Grimm*
Illustration and text by Mike Peters

GRIMMY from *Mother Goose and Grimm*
Illustration and text by Mike Peters

GRIMMY from *Mother Goose and Grimm*
Illustration and text by Mike Peters

Pomegranate

BOX 6099, ROHNERT PARK, CA 94927

GRIMMY from *Mother Goose and Grimm*
Illustration and text by Mike Peters

Pomegranate

BOX 6099, ROHNERT PARK, CA 94927

GRIMMY from *Mother Goose and Grimm*
Illustration and text by Mike Peters

Pomegranate

BOX 6099, ROHNERT PARK, CA 94927

GRIMMY from *Mother Goose and Grimm*
Illustration and text by Mike Peters

Pomegranate BOX 6099, ROHNERT PARK, CA 94927

GRIMMY from *Mother Goose and Grimm*
Illustration and text by Mike Peters

Pomegranate BOX 6099, ROHNERT PARK, CA 94927

GRIMMY from *Mother Goose and Grimm*
Illustration and text by Mike Peters

Pomegranate BOX 6099, ROHNERT PARK, CA 94927

GRIMMY from *Mother Goose and Grimm*
Illustration and text by Mike Peters

Pomegranate

BOX 6099, ROHNERT PARK, CA 94927

GRIMMY from *Mother Goose and Grimm*
Illustration and text by Mike Peters

Pomegranate

BOX 6099, ROHNERT PARK, CA 94927

GRIMMY from *Mother Goose and Grimm*
Illustration and text by Mike Peters

GRIMMY from *Mother Goose and Grimm*
Illustration and text by Mike Peters

Pomegranate   BOX 6099, ROHNERT PARK, CA 94927

GRIMMY from *Mother Goose and Grimm*
Illustration and text by Mike Peters

GRIMMY from *Mother Goose and Grimm*
Illustration and text by Mike Peters

BOX 6099, ROHNERT PARK, CA 94927

Pomegranate

GRIMMY from *Mother Goose and Grimm*
Illustration and text by Mike Peters

Pomegranate   BOX 6099, ROHNERT PARK, CA 94927

GRIMMY from *Mother Goose and Grimm*
Illustration and text by Mike Peters

Pomegranate BOX 6099, ROHNERT PARK, CA 94927